NLP

Acquire The Ability To Regulate Your Actions, Thoughts, And Emotions By Harnessing The Force Of Your Cognitive Processes

("The Definitive Handbook On Neuro-linguistic Programming)

Clint Vogel

TABLE OF CONTENT

Fundamental Principles Of Natural Language Processing 1

The Influence Of Words 36

Objective Reality Vs. Subjective World 59

Framing Techniques 65

Psychological Influence Through Neuro-Linguistic Programming For Fostering And Enhancing Romantic Partnerships 84

The Potential Transformation Of Your Life Through NLP 97

Brainwashing Techniques 104

What Factors Contribute To Your Inability To Achieve Weight Loss? 119

Metaphors In ZeNLP ! 143

Fundamental Principles Of Natural Language Processing

What is NLP ?

Neurolinguistic Programming (NLP) serves as a comprehensive communication model that offers intricate insights into human behavior. It imparts knowledge regarding the processes we undertake and the internal strategies we employ to evoke specific emotions such as happiness, sadness, elation, or anger, which subsequently spur our actions and ultimately lead us to attain a particular outcome, as opposed to an alternative one.

It serves as a model rather than a theory, and thus its objective is to accurately depict successful practices without generating theories or establishing connections with psychological or philosophical systems or approaches.

One aspect of this premise is that by acquiring knowledge of the subconscious strategies employed by successful individuals, we can consciously adopt and implement those techniques in order to attain success in our professional endeavors or emotional well-being.

Natural Language Processing (NLP) possesses a repertoire of tools and techniques aimed at cultivating states of exceptional proficiency in communication, thereby eliciting transformations. Throughout the subsequent pages, we shall examine its impact on individuals as well as its applicability to others.

Significant tenets of NLP within the scope of human nature

Initially, natural language processing (NLP) researchers focused their study on highly proficient therapists. Fritz Perls, the pioneer of Gestalt therapy emphasizing the concept of "being present in the moment," stands among the initial therapists subjected to rigorous examination. Proficient in deciphering nonverbal cues and adept at rapidly gathering insights from individuals, he possessed an innate talent in this regard.

He dedicated his attention to the antithesis of psychoanalysis, which demanded prolonged effort and personal inquiry in order to apprehend the intricate nature of human development.

Virginia Satir, the second therapist under study, was instrumental in the development of family therapy in her field. Her commitment lay in addressing the challenges within the entire family structure, rather than exclusively focusing on a single individual with issues.

He asserted that each behavior and action comprised an integral component of the familial dynamic. He ascertained that by solely addressing an individual, the dynamics of the family would continually revert him back to the identical predicament, thereby emphasizing the significance of engaging with the entire family unit.

Milton Erickson, a physician renowned for his development of clinical hypnotherapy, was the third individual examined by the pioneers in the field of NLP . Distinguished from Perls and Satir by his distinctive approach, Erickson's remarkable achievements seemed almost miraculous, revealing him to be a highly gifted genius.

Another individual, known as Moshe Feldenkrais, possessed the ability to facilitate bodily healing through a remarkable manual therapy technique executed with his hands.

The fundamental operating principles of NLP , referred to as "presuppositions," demonstrate the core unifying beliefs held by the four key individuals who were examined in order to uncover the most efficacious approach, ultimately serving as the bedrock of NLP .

Consensus was reached among all of these experts regarding the fundamental tenets concerning the nature of humanity. We shall enumerate two fundamental tenets. The initial option is:

An internal adversary does not exist. No domestic foe can be found. There is an absence of an internal nemesis. The presence of an internal enemy is non-existent.

There is no tangible entity residing within you that manifests opposition against your existence. Those beliefs where you feel that you are broken or with an internal enemy, you can take them out of yourself. Individuals engage in self-destructive behaviors, such as excessive alcohol consumption or violent criminal activities, driven by their conviction that these actions are indispensable.

Certain behaviors may appear irrational to the majority, however, it is crucial to comprehend an individual's unique perspective and thought process, as it ultimately shapes their actions.

The second principle asserts:

Every behavior carries a positive underlying intention." "Each behavior is driven by a positive motive." "There is a positive purpose behind every behavior." "Behind every action lies a positive intention.

Consider an illustrative scenario wherein you personally encounter an individual, and subsequently experience phenomena such as trembling legs and a quivering voice. What are the underlying reasons for such occurrences? There is no inherent flaw within you; rather, it is your mindset that suggests potential harm when encountering this individual. Your mind acts as a sentinel, ensuring your survival through these cautionary signals, thereby deterring any form of confrontation.

By utilizing NLP , one has the ability to examine the inner workings of the mind in order to discern the underlying pattern that gives rise to a specific response, subsequently employing strategies to modify said pattern.

Please be aware that there is no internal adversary that opposes you, and that every action is driven by a well-intentioned motive. Your cognitive processes currently function optimally within your current framework, but it may be beneficial to consider potential refinements, considering that the majority of brains are wired during the developmental period between 2 and 5 years. Without modifying the foundational programming that was established during that time, we are likely to perpetuate familiar behavioral patterns unconsciously and without much awareness.

Individuals possess the innate capabilities necessary for achieving success.

What measures should we undertake to attain success?

Many individuals frequently contend that their lack of certain attributes or resources prevents them from achieving success. If I were to possess greater wealth, a younger age, a broader range of experiences, a higher level of education, stronger connections, and so forth, it is highly likely that I would achieve success. They possess a multitude of rationales that, in actuality, lack validity.

Let's say money. In order to generate an income, one must possess financial capital. Do you frequently encounter such utterances? Observe the comprehensive compilation of the wealthiest individuals globally. Many among them have attained their fortunes beginning from a point of minimal or even negative net worth. Money should not be used as a justification.

What about education? Similarly! Take another look at the roster of the wealthiest individuals. The majority of them did not acquire college degrees, and it is conceivable that many did not even complete high school. Pejorative opinions sometimes circulate, suggesting that affluent individuals are merely individuals lacking intelligence who simply employ highly educated professionals. Have you encountered such expressions before? Indeed, this statement holds true.

Additionally, certain individuals employ their connections as a pretext. If, indeed, you do not possess a connection, you have the option to establish one. In this regard, attending the same location as the individuals you seek to connect with, such as a seminar, may prove beneficial. While attending a seminar, in addition to acquiring new knowledge, I consistently take the initiative to introduce myself and establish professional connections. Broaden your network by becoming a member of various communities. Just that simple!

Subsequently, certain individuals employ time as a justification. I am deemed ineligible due to my age. I am deemed ineligible due to my age. However, history has shown us that attainment of success is not bound by age limitations. Esteemed individuals such as Gordon Bowker, Ray Kroc, John Pemberton, and Colonel Harland David Sanders have demonstrated that one's chronological age should not deter them from pursuing and achieving success. And the aforementioned individuals, namely Perenna Kei, Mark Zuckerberg, Drew Houston, Evan Spiegel, and Farrah Gray, possess the understanding that youthfulness is advantageous.

Even individuals with disabilities employing them as a justification. We are aware that a considerable number of individuals with disabilities have achieved significant accomplishments in society. Physical disability should not be regarded as a justification, as evidenced by the exceptional achievements of individuals such as Anthony Robles, Bobby Martin, Vinod Thakur, Xu Yuehua, and notably, Nick Vujicic.

Ah, fortuity! Triumph and luck are inextricably intertwined. Kindly acquaint yourself with the biographies of Abraham Lincoln, Soichiro Honda, and Nelson Mandela, as their narratives are characterized by more than mere fortune or chance.

What sets successful individuals apart from the average person? What measures do we need to undertake to attain success?

People possess the requisite internal capacities necessary for success. We possess the capabilities needed to attain and accomplish success. All endeavors originate internally, devoid of external influence. Any triumph that one aspires to attain, every necessity that one requires, resides within their own being. It is through the utilization of the tremendous capabilities of the brain and mind that such accomplishments are realized.

You have the potential to attain various accomplishments, both on a professional and personal level, by channeling the capacities of your intellect and cognition. This book aims to facilitate your acquisition of techniques rooted in NLP , enabling you to harness the cognitive and intellectual potential of your brain and mind to successfully reach your objectives. You will:

1. Exhibit improved self-restraint.

2. Provoke the desired emotional state.

3. Efface undesirable emotions, including phobias.

4. Eliminate self-imposed limitations and choices.

5. Emulate the success patterns demonstrated by exceptional individuals.

6. Establish a rapport or cultivate a relationship expeditiously.

7. Comprehend the concept of transformation.

Inception

During the 1970s, John Grinder and Richard Bandler, esteemed pioneers of neurolinguistic programming, endeavored to develop precise frameworks representing the highest achievable levels of human proficiency. In their initial partnership, the joint effort resulted in the publication titled The Structure of Magic, wherein the authors discerned the behavioral and verbal patterns exhibited by two esteemed colleagues, namely Virginia Satir and Fritz Perls. The forthcoming joint project of these individuals revolves around the study and investigation of the Patterns of Hypnotic Techniques as pioneered by Milton H. Erickson performed an analysis on the behavioral and linguistic tendencies of Erickson, a distinguished psychiatrist.

Upon their fortuitous encounter, Bandler, an esteemed warehouse assistant at Science and Behavioral Books, and Pucelik, an honorable veteran of the Vietnam War beset by trauma, collectively concluded that they would mutually assist one another in the arduous task of reconstructing their respective lives. Bandler's affiliation with a publishing company facilitated the replication of the techniques documented in the transcripts and tapes, particularly those attributed to Fritz Perls, the renowned pioneer of Gestalt Therapy. At the outset, their sole objective was to enhance their quality of life.

Following their discovery of Perls' written works, Bandler and Pucelik initiated the application of Gestalt Therapy within a group setting at the esteemed University of California, Santa

Cruz (UCSC). In due course, John Grinder, a budding professor of linguistics at UCSC, joined their ranks. Grinder's astute observations and thought-provoking inquiries heralded the commencement of an enduring and triumphant collaboration among the trio, ultimately culminating in the inception of neuro-linguistic programming. They employed their combined expertise and ingenuity to scrutinize and form conceptual representations of the contributions made by Perls, in addition to Virginia Satir, a pioneering figure in the field of family therapy. They sought to replicate the research conducted by Perls and Satir in order to comprehend the factors underlying their accomplishments. Subsequently, they were acquainted with the literary contributions of Milton Erickson, an eminent psychiatrist renowned for his expertise in medical hypnosis and family therapy.

Grinder and Bandler, through their preliminary efforts, made significant contributions to and systematized their methodologies and discoveries, eventually designating it as "Neurolinguistic Programming." Their purpose was to embody the interconnectedness of the brain, body, and linguistic systems.

Over the course of time, experts have honed their expertise in NLP , thereby cultivating additional techniques and resources for effective communication and personal transformation. During the 1990s, there emerged a subsequent wave of NLP that directed its attention towards matters concerning identity, mission, and vision. Ever since the mid-1970s, Neuro-Linguistic Programming (NLP) has attained global recognition and significantly enhanced the quality of numerous individuals' lives. Its efficacy has been particularly demonstrated in various esteemed professional domains, including sales, counseling and psychotherapy, law, management, creative arts, health, and education.

What Is NLP ?

Neurolinguistic Programming (NLP) can be deconstructed into three fundamental elements that govern the human experience: Neurology, Language, and Programming. The Neurological system governs bodily functions, Language serves as the means through which we communicate with both ourselves and others, and Programming pertains to the intricately designed models and systems that exist within our world. What is the anticipated outcome resulting from a provided input? NLP demonstrates the profound interrelation among our cognitive faculty (Neuro), communication patterns (Linguistic), and patterns of conduct (Programming).

CHAPTER 2
Varied Outlooks on the Dark Triad

The dark triad, as previously mentioned, might have piqued your interest, thus leading to your desire for further knowledge on the subject. Should this be the situation, then you are heading in the correct direction. In the present chapter, an exploration is undertaken to ascertain the distinct impacts exerted by the individuals comprising the dark triad upon individuals across various domains. Above all, we address these issues within the professional setting, wherein they tend to be prevalent and detrimentally impact the overall performance of the organization. As you continue, it is imperative to grasp the paramount significance of comprehending the impact that each dark personality exhibits on the organization, as they possess the proclivity to influence the organization's baseline in distinct ways.

The Dark Triad

A correlation exists between the dark triad traits and the attainment of leadership roles as well as interpersonal influence. We discuss more below:

In the workplace:

Machiavellianism

The phenomenon of Machiavellianism in professional settings has piqued the curiosity of numerous psychologists. Machiavellianism, along with the other facets of the dark triad, exerts an impact on the dynamics within the professional environment. The workplace encompasses a paradigm incorporating the Machiavellian model.

Maintenance of power
Aggressive strategies employed by the management.
Manipulative behaviors.

Individuals who achieve high scores on the Machiavellianism spectrum demonstrate elevated levels of charisma, which often results in advantageous leadership capabilities in specific domains. Furthermore, the association of their participation within organizations has been connected to deleterious workplace conduct.

It is acknowledged that individuals inclined towards Machiavellianism exhibit a higher tendency to engage in falsehoods during interview situations, demonstrating a greater degree of willingness to do so. Therefore, in the context of Machiavellianism, it is improbable to obtain truthful responses during an interview. They possess more pronounced inclinations that may compel them towards deceit during interviews in comparison to other qualities within the triad. Furthermore, what exacerbates the situation is their belief that engaging in deception during interviews is acceptable. It is probable that they will employ diverse strategies with the intention of exerting influence over the interviewers in a manner favorable to them. Individuals with Machiavellian tendencies have an increased propensity to fabricate information regarding their personal attributes during interviews, thereby exhibiting a limited receptiveness towards the interviewer's guidance in shaping interview content.

Individuals who exhibit Machiavellian traits often engage in strategic manipulation and exploitation in professional settings, with the primary objective of furthering their own personal interests and exerting control and authority over their peers. These principles serve as the foundational beliefs for this collective of individuals:

Never express humility.
It is of greater efficacy to approach interactions with others in an arrogant manner.
Ethical and moral principles are neither inherent nor will they ever be ingrained within their character. These items are being taken into consideration for the duration of the week. They possess the entitlement to engage in falsehood, fraud, and manipulation as they judge to be suitable.
Their preference is to command fear rather than cultivate affection from others.

A few of the measures they might adopt within the work setting encompass:

Failing to fulfill the duty of communicating crucial information
Engaging in the dissemination of unfounded rumors about a colleague.
Not fulfilling job responsibilities.
And subtly undermining others' reputation with management.

Consequently, research indicates a direct association between office harassment and the Machiavellian personality trait. Consequently, the experience of bullying demonstrates a negative correlation with the perceptions of organizational adhocracy and a stronger association with perceptions of hierarchical culture. This concept exhibited a correlation with the occurrence of abusive supervision towards subordinates.
Narcissism

Narcissism in the professional setting has a detrimental impact on an organization, as individuals with this trait are inclined to exhibit counterproductive work behaviors when their sense of self-importance is challenged. This specific characteristic may also be categorized as a personality disorder.

During job interviews, members of this triad often demonstrate exceptional performance, resulting in more favorable hiring evaluations compared to their non-triad peers. The level of cunning employed by them is often so remarkable that even seasoned and adept evaluators may inadvertently overlook it. One potential explanation for their higher ratings could be attributed to the distinctive nature of interviews, setting them apart from other social scenarios. Consider it in this manner.

During an interview, it is permissible to confidently present one's achievements in order to establish a favorable perception.

Narcissistic individuals utilize this platform as an opportunity to upstage their colleagues. These individuals possess a remarkable aptitude for exhibiting behaviors that generate favorable perceptions, thereby facilitating the establishment of positive impressions, irrespective of their lack of intent to sustain satisfactory job performance in the foreseeable future. Hence, it is plausible to conclude that upon your first encounter with a narcissist in a professional setting, you are inclined to perceive them as amiable, emotionally stable, proficient, and captivating. They exhibit a preference for tidy and flamboyant attire, execute confident physical gestures, and demonstrate amiable facial gestures. Regrettably, the favorable news for them is invariably ephemeral, as their allure quickly diminishes.

Narcissistic individuals exert an influence on the levels of stress experienced, the rates of absenteeism, and the occurrence of staff turnover within organizational settings. Individuals who are employed and have regular interactions with individuals displaying narcissistic traits experience elevated levels of stress. Narcissism exhibits a strong correlation with interpersonal aggression, disruptive actions towards the efforts of others, as well as the inefficient utilization of time and resources of fellow individuals. The implementation of such antagonistic workplace protocols gives rise to elevated stress levels among employees, subsequently leading to increased rates of staff absenteeism and turnover.

In order for individuals with narcissistic tendencies to flourish, they require a continual source of validation and attention. For example, a manager displaying narcissistic tendencies will possess both material resources and human resources that will endure his self-centered behavior. Inanimate entities typically encompass devices, office scenery, and vehicles, whereas animate sources of attention involve coworkers and associates. On occasion, team members may provide assistance and subsequently realize that their aid turns into continuous provision unless appropriate boundaries are upheld. A manager characterized by narcissism frequently safeguards their supply networks in order to impede the process of objective decision-making. Managers of this kind frequently assess the merits of long-term strategies based on the quantum of personal advantage they stand to derive, rather than considering the benefits accrued to the organization.

In addition, individuals with narcissistic traits often display a preference for hierarchical structures, perceiving them as opportunities to ascend to higher positions where they can acquire advantages such as authority and prestige. They have a strong desire to attain elevated positions within an organization and possess superior proficiency in achieving this objective. Therefore, they will not be present in an environment characterized by low prospects for advancement. They will be concerned with their public image and the reception of compliments, rather than focusing on the stakeholders' best interests. Insufficient research has been conducted to comprehensively comprehend the impact of narcissism on an organization, despite the potential advantages associated with certain narcissistic tendencies.

Occasionally, instances of corporate narcissism arise. This scenario occurs when a narcissistic individual ascends the hierarchical ladder and assumes a position of senior management, such as a Chief Executive Officer (CEO) or a leadership role. In this capacity, they are able to procure a suitable ensemble of co-dependents who dutifully provide them with the requisite attention that fulfills their narcissistic tendencies. While they may ostensibly declare their affection for the organization, it is fundamentally apparent that their loyalty primarily lies with their own personal objectives. That is the reason why it can be observed that individuals of this nature are capable of operating financially prosperous businesses, albeit with an unethical foundation. In order to differentiate a well-functioning organization from a dysfunctional one, it would be advantageous to evaluate the organization's capacity to prevent the appointment of individuals with narcissistic tendencies to key leadership positions.

In regard to workplace bullying, individuals with narcissistic tendencies exhibit a predisposition towards employing indirect tactics, including but not limited to: disregarding or dismissing an individual, deliberately withholding pertinent information that may impact one's ability to perform, persistently reminding someone of their errors, disseminating harmful rumors, and assigning tasks that do not align with an individual's skill level. They display a disinclination towards employing direct approaches such as intimidation, raising their voices, making baseless allegations, and engaging in criticism of their subordinates. Individuals with narcissistic tendencies are prone to displaying heightened levels of aggression and confrontation, as these tendencies are commonly associated with low levels of self-esteem. When engaging in bullying behavior, the typical outcome entails a sense of gratification experienced subsequent to the event. Typically, they have a propensity to evade tasks while exhibiting no qualms about appropriating someone else's work in any capacity. Furthermore, it is worth noting that they possess a penchant for manipulation, as you are likely aware of their affiliation with the triad. Within the professional setting, they frequently manipulate circumstances to unjustly take credit for achievements within the organization that they had no involvement in.

The Influence Of Words

When we exert influence over another individual, prompting them to undertake a specific course of action or arrive at a particular decision, it begs the question: what precise actions or mechanisms enable this outcome to transpire? Do we effectively emit cerebral waves or signals into the Cosmos that relay information about the actions one would undertake? Certainly, it is feasible to provide guidance to another individual through direct communication. You make a request of someone, and that individual complies with it. Indeed, it can be considered a means of exerting influence over an individual, albeit with their voluntary commitment to fulfill any tasks or demands you may present. One can exert influence upon another individual to compel them into performing a specific action through the utilization of blackmail or threats. There is a diverse range of potential outcomes that can arise when influencing another individual to engage in an action according to your preferences, encompassing both favorable and unfavorable consequences. What if you possess the capability to accomplish this while remaining completely incognito to the involved individuals?

The overwhelming majority of our activities and decisions stem from various collaborations and interactions with others. This does not account for minor decisions that we make on a daily basis and the mundane tasks we perform as part of our daily routines. This topic does not encompass matters concerning television programming choices and the appropriate timing for accessing such content. Included in this are the majority of the significant decisions that you, along with others, will undertake on a daily basis. These decisions encompass both professional and personal spheres. We frequently amalgamate without fully acknowledging it. This is predominantly due to the fact that we, as individuals, possess an inherent inclination towards social interaction, stemming from our fundamental nature. Collectively, we strive for mutual satisfaction and fulfillment through our collaborative efforts.

Please take note of the following. Engaging in manipulative behavior through negative tactics inevitably eradicates any potential for establishing a positive relationship with that individual in perpetuity. You shall be regarded as a hostile entity. Indeed, whilst it may be possible to instill a sense of fear and thereby attain a certain measure of dominion over an individual, the ultimate consequence will invariably prove adverse. If you opt to execute your plan employing constructive strategies, you have the potential to achieve comparable results while also acquiring additional benefits for future purposes. Having connections in influential roles can greatly contribute to one's success. In this scenario, the attributes of having fortitude, attentiveness, and a holistic perspective become crucial.

An additional point to bear in mind is that we are not accountable for the actions of others. Each individual bears the responsibility for their own decisions and, ultimately, they are the ones accountable for the choices they make. Regardless of the level of proficiency in manipulation, an individual will always be unable to dictate someone else's choices. As individuals adept in influence, our utmost capability lies in guiding those individuals towards their own discernment. Please bear in mind this crucial aspect as well. In order to exert influence over someone, it is necessary to persuade them into perceiving their choice as indispensable and to instill the belief that they themselves are the sole architects of the decision-making process. This aspect holds paramount significance in acquiring the skills of influencing individuals.

The final crucial factor, particularly pertinent within the professional environment, entails distinguishing between the acts of manipulation and persuasion. The two terms are employed interchangeably, however, they possess dissimilar characteristics. A manipulative individual often exhibits heightened assertiveness and demands less from their targeted subjects. Additionally, in the context of negative or injurious intentions, the prevalence of manipulation tends to outweigh the utilization of persuasion techniques. Manipulation frequently encompasses tactics such as intimidation and coercion. The outcomes of this phenomenon generally tend to be adverse, often resulting in detrimental consequences. Persuasion entails a more dynamic and reciprocal approach, often yielding more favorable results. Individuals who employ the tactic of persuasion rely on the active involvement and general awareness of the subjects they aim to influence.

This can be likened to a mentor-protégé dynamic. The fundamental distinction between persuasion and manipulation lies in the intention of the individual involved, solely aiming for the optimal outcome that benefits all parties.

As is the case with any other proficiency that is not universally possessed, there exist guiding principles pertaining to the art of persuasion. Principles hold significant and congruent worth. An absence of moral values results in an individual who is petty and detrimental to the well-being of others. Let us examine a few of them and analyze their applicability. Your powers of influence are not a form of manipulation. It is crucial to bear in mind that there exists a substantial disparity between these two concepts, and the majority of individuals harbor an aversion towards engagement in manipulative behavior. This pertains to the individuals engaging in the activity rather than the recipients of said activity.

That is effectively influencing those who can be influenced. This implies the necessity of carefully choosing your topic, identifying an appropriate individual to influence, and ensuring that the timing is optimal. The significance of context cannot be underestimated. Please bear in mind the following information. In order for an individual to be convinced, it is imperative that they possess a genuine interest. Should they lack interest, it will prove exceedingly difficult to sway their opinion. Consider a student in an educational institution who lacks focus. The child is not comprehending or assimilating any of the information taught in class. The instructor is endeavoring, or ought to be endeavoring, to impart knowledge to the student; however, due to lack of engagement, the student is not acquiring knowledge.

There exists a fundamental principle known as "reciprocity compels," which points to the innate inclination of humans to reciprocate gestures of kindness and favor. This is where the principle of mutual exchange comes into action. Another is persistence pays. This should be considered a matter of basic rationale. I was once informed about an anecdote involving a fish that happened to be confined within a fisherman's receptacle.

The fish consistently exhibited a behavior of propelling itself out of the vessel and onto the surface. Having repeated this action multiple times, the fisherman eventually returned the fish to its natural habitat within the pond. An additional principle entails being genuine in offering compliments and refraining from falsehood. Don't assume anything either. Make consistent efforts to establish a positive and meaningful connection with the individual. This will yield considerable advantages. It is exceedingly difficult to convince individuals without establishing a sense of rapport. It is feasible to manipulate, yet not to effectively convince or sway.

Additional tenets involve the generation of scarcity. "Act promptly and make your way as there is a limited stock remaining!" This is a line commonly featured in television advertisements for automobiles. In addition to this, it is imperative to establish clear expectations, especially when navigating interactions with others rather than focusing solely on oneself. It is imperative that you comprehend the rationale underlying their expectations. Behavioral adaptability and the transference of energy are necessitated. One must endeavor to inspire and invigorate others rather than deplete them of their vitality. Refrain from going to an excessive extent and exhibiting spasmodic behavior. It is imperative to ensure effective and articulate verbal communication skills. This creates an impression of intellectual acumen, exemplary work ethics, and extensive expertise. Furthermore, acquire the ability to exude confidence and abstain from conveying any sense of timidity or self-doubt.

Now, let us examine the key competencies required to achieve mastery in manipulation or persuasion. Each of these necessitates a distinct set of skills. Both necessitate a significant level of intellectual capacity. If you lack the intellectual acumen to comprehend your objective and the prevailing circumstances, it would be prudent to relinquish your pursuit. Being cognizant of our surroundings, or practicing mindfulness, is integral to achieving success. An additional variant of requisite intelligence pertains to the concept of emotional intelligence. The individual engaging in persuasion must possess proficiency in this particular form of intelligence.

Possessing assertiveness is also an admirable attribute. Individuals who possess a proclivity towards reticence or a dislike for contentious situations typically lack the ability to effectively steer others. If one struggles to effectively guide oneself, one's ability to effectively lead others is compromised. This is a manifestation of sound logical reasoning. Moreover, it is imperative to demonstrate forbearance and possess the capacity to observe from a distance. Individuals lacking patience tend to struggle when it comes to effectively persuading or manipulating others. This arises from the fact that the procedure typically necessitates a certain amount of time and care. Unless you intend to wield a weapon and direct it towards the person whom you wish to instruct, necessitating their compliance, it will be imperative to allow yourself a sufficient timeframe to accomplish the task. Please bear in mind that the decision is not within your purview. The responsibility for the creation lies with the other individual, and your role is solely to guide them in that direction.

Charisma is important too. It is important for you to project yourself as an amiable individual. We often exhibit a tendency to align ourselves and concur with individuals whom we harbor positive sentiments towards. Take politicians, for example. One of the primary attributes that a politician endeavors to exhibit is affability. "I'm a nice guy. Indeed, I embody trustworthiness and diligent work ethic, while also possessing an amicable disposition. Please consider casting your vote for me based on your affinities towards my character and qualities. This sentiment may ring familiar, wouldn't you agree? That politician has embarked on the endeavor of persuasion. The individual in question is endeavoring to persuade you to cast your vote in their favor.

The aforementioned traits serve as the fundamental foundations alongside the strategies of manipulation and persuasion. Similar to other regulations, there exist exceptions; however, a proficient manipulator must primarily possess attributes of intelligence, charisma, and assertiveness. Subsequently, the individual must integrate the three elements and subsequently employ them with meticulousness and perseverance. To effectively manipulate, one must possess knowledge and understanding of the subject. Once again, the individual in question is exercising autonomy in their decision-making process.

As the orchestrator, it is incumbent upon you to persuade that individual in such a way that they perceive it to be in their utmost advantage. Unless one resorts to petty tactics, such as blackmail, the possession of the aforementioned three qualities becomes superfluous. The sole requirement for an individual engaging in blackmail is. It comprises the information, or armament, that he intends to utilize. This does not necessitate any level of expertise. It solely necessitates the capacity to exhibit apathy towards others.

Improving Social Connections

As elucidated in the chapter dedicated to mirroring, gaining comprehension of NLP has the potential to facilitate the establishment of more robust connections with individuals who hold significance in your life, as well as fostering new alliances with individuals whom you desire to embrace into your life. During your future interactions with others, it may prove beneficial to incorporate the technique of subtle mirroring into your verbal and non-verbal communication. Additionally, one can assess the level of engagement of their conversation partner by discreetly providing them with opportunities to mimic their own changes in posture or pace of conversation.

Strengthening Romantic Relationships

As elucidated in the dedicated chapter pertaining to submodalities, the field of NLP enables us to comprehensively grasp our optimal reactions to manifestations of affection. Conveying this information to your partner has the potential to enhance interpersonal connections and foster confidence. On the other hand, through an effort to comprehend your partner's favored submodality, you can enhance your ability to express affection towards them more efficiently. Directing attention to the medium that will elicit the greatest impact amplifies the efficacy of every gesture.

Altering Your Financial Relationship

Applying natural language processing techniques to alter your belief system regarding wealth can yield significant outcomes in your financial endeavors. One instance wherein appreciating the transformation of your mindset, moving away from the notion of perpetually relying on each paycheck and embracing the prospect of skillfully managing your expenditures and generating a financial cushion, can yield profound repercussions in one's life. Despite facing financial constraints, possessing the knowledge of how to reframe fiscal challenges can considerably enhance their manageability. The previous perception of an incessant battle to meet financial obligations can be redefined as an exclusive prospect and endeavor to acquire the skills of leading a more fulfilling life within limited expenditure. It presents a remarkable occasion to direct attention towards the invaluable aspects of life that come without a monetary price, namely family, friends, and experiences, which hold significant importance. For those individuals who are entrepreneurs, altering restrictive beliefs regarding our aptitude to expand business concepts and generate substantial income can serve as the crucial element in advancing your business to a higher echelon.

Building Powerful Habits

Employing Natural Language Processing (NLP) and techniques such as the swish method can facilitate the rewiring of unfavorable habits, transforming them into constructive habits that are congruent with our life objectives. Being capable of identifying the underlying factors that contribute to behaviors such as procrastination, argumentativeness, excessive eating, and so on, and subsequently modifying the triggers to facilitate the adoption of preferred behaviors. Implementing this approach to cultivate a small number of impactful habits instead of harmful ones can result in significant transformative effects on our lives.

Improving Health

In a similar vein, possessing the knowledge of employing NLP techniques to establish anchors and regulate routines can significantly elevate your state of well-being. Maintaining good health requires a long-term commitment, rather than a short-term effort, and it encompasses a continuous way of life rather than sporadic actions. If we can cultivate authentic enthusiasm towards endeavors that enhance our well-being, whilst eliminating impediments and patterns that hinder our progress, we can attain the desired lifestyle we seek.

Having Better Organization

Experiencing a lack of organization is a prevalent challenge that is often accompanied by deeply entrenched negative perceptions held by many individuals. I am inherently prone to a lack of organization. I will perpetually struggle to maintain organization in my office/living space. Utilizing natural language processing (NLP) to comprehend the root causes of your disarray can empower you to cultivate novel practices of orderly storage instead of haphazardly discarding objects. NLP possesses the capacity to reconfigure one's belief systems, resulting in the development of a profound inner assurance that one is adept at maintaining organization and orderliness in life.

Making Clearer Decisions

Establishing stable references that elicit sensations of lucidity and tranquility equips you with the capacity to restore your mental clarity amidst moments when your discernment becomes obscured. Frequently, our most unfavorable choices are made when overwhelmed by anger or frustration, and possessing the knowledge to surmount these emotions through the utilization of an effective anchor or content reframe can fundamentally transform our capacity to act prudently. Additionally, actively practicing future pacing before embarking on a project that is expected to entail numerous similar situations can equip you with the skills to effectively navigate difficult scenarios and maintain composure in high-pressure situations.

Increasing Self-appreciation

The utilization of NLP for transforming negative beliefs into positive ones presents an entirely novel prospect for identifying aspects of oneself that are worthy of appreciation. By suppressing your internal critic, you will foster affirmative contemplation of your abilities, distinctive attributes, and notable aspects that set you apart in life.

Improving Self-confidence

By dismantling negative beliefs and actively envisioning a successful future, one can cultivate a profound sense of preparedness to confront various challenges that may arise throughout their endeavors. Self-doubt often arises from insufficient preparation, and addressing this issue can be achieved through diligent practice and thorough envisioning of prospective situations.

Objective Reality Vs. Subjective World

An exemplary instance of a theoretical conjecture involves posing the following hypothetical inquiry: If one were to cast a stone into a tranquil body of water, would it initiate undulations within the liquid? The objective truth in this situation is that, indeed, the stone did create undulations in the water. The objective viewpoint does not rely on the presence of anyone or the necessity of an observer witnessing the act of someone throwing the stone in order for the occurrence to be considered factual. An objective statement remains entirely impartial. It remains unaffected by an individual's personal experiences or subjective inclinations. It can be substantiated and grounded in factual evidence.

Nevertheless, adherents of NLP and comparable ideologies hold the perspective that an individual's apprehension of actuality is regulated by their senses, thereby indicating the absence or rarity of an objective reality that can be comprehended. Henceforth, all aspects of existence are subject to individual interpretation. Our shared reality is shaped by the subjective experiences and perceptions that we collectively construct as members of society. Hence, a subjective statement considers the demeanor, sentiments, and visual indications of the speaker, which are impervious to substantiation through factual or statistical evidence.

OBJECTIVE REALITY: Envision, if you will, a scenario where you find yourself positioned in close proximity to a building that stands at a height equivalent to eight stories. The authenticity of the building may be confirmed by any individual observing it firsthand, being in close proximity to it, or capturing its image using a smartphone. Fundamentally, objective reality entails a compilation of entities that we can ascertain to inherently exist, regardless of our subjective existence. In essence, each one of us possesses the capability to validate every facet of objective reality. Similarly, the nonexistence of said structure would indicate that it does not pertain to the realm of actuality.

Each individual among us possesses a significant stake in comprehending the nature of objective reality. For instance, individuals in the profession of selling automobiles (or any other sales profession, although we will focus on car dealers) often have a propensity to embellish the exceptional qualities of their vehicles. However, as a customer, we desire to ascertain the genuine objective attributes of the vehicle. We might seek advice from an acquaintance or peruse a pamphlet to acquire this information. However diligent our efforts may be in comprehending all the constituents of the objective reality, its foundation will invariably rest upon assumptions.

It proves challenging to verify the elements of objective reality. In our formative years, we were all acquainted with the tales of Santa Claus or the Easter Bunny. We held the conviction that these narratives upheld the truth (and consequently corresponded to objective reality), but subsequently discovered that they were indeed unfounded. Consider, for example, individuals specializing in divination and esoteric practices. There exist individuals across the globe who profess to have witnessed apparitions of deceased relatives from prior times, experienced auditory perception of the voices of departed loved ones, or observed inanimate objects such as tables or chairs exhibiting inexplicable movements. All assertions can be subjected to examination through the interrogation of witnesses, the utilization of surveillance equipment, or the meticulous scrutiny aimed at ascertaining if the fortune teller is employing deceptive techniques, such as sleight of hand, or any other form of trickery to deceive their clientele. Regrettably, there has never been substantiated documentation or evidence to validate any assertions regarding actual sightings of deceased loved ones in a verifiably objective manner. Naturally, there exist individuals who hold beliefs in mystics; however, whenever these beliefs are subject to scrutiny, the outcomes remain speculative and inconclusive. It is commonly assumed that these beliefs provide individuals with hope and solace, or possess some other subjective value, although they are deficient in discerning between objective reality and the realm of subjectivity.

The phenomenon of subjectivity revolves around the perception and interpretation of individuals in relation to their sensory experiences of reality.

Framing Techniques

Framing techniques employed in the field of NLP typically synergize effectively with numerous complementary strategies. Framing serves to enhance or diminish emotional states by reconstructing pathways within the primal limbic region of the brain, specifically facilitating communication between the amygdala and hippocampus.

Prior to delving into the particulars of implementing framing techniques, it is prudent to first ascertain the emotional frames of reference with which we are confronted. Individuals have a tendency to acquire knowledge and attribute significance to occurrences based on the circumstances surrounding those particular situations. Conversely, it is important to consider our recollections explicitly related to those individuals.

Upon thoughtful consideration, it becomes evident that both the recollections of past experiences and the envisioned possibilities of future events are akin to a compilation of images, comparable to the film negatives seen in antiquated movie projectors. They represent mere glimpses of occurrences to which we subsequently assign significance. Nevertheless, it is worth noting that individuals often fail to recognize that the significance or emotional attachment they attribute to something might not be precise and is subject to alteration.

You may be acquainted with the popular adage that goes "If something rings true to you, then it holds true." This entails the proposition of translating reality into the external realm, and constitutes primarily an observation within the field of quantum mechanics. It undoubtedly holds immense veracity in the realm of personal experiences, particularly pertaining to sentiments and emotions. The cognitive process entails the storage of long-term memory data by the hippocampus, concomitantly with the amygdala generating the corresponding emotional response.

Despite their close anatomical proximity, these two regions must establish communication in order to generate a comprehensive understanding of the event, encompassing the associated emotions and meanings. Occasionally, their judgment in this matter may be flawed, or alternatively, you have the opportunity to modify this connection if it does not align with your preferences or, to be more precise, your emotional response.

Chapter 3—Exerting Influence on Others using Neuro-Linguistic Programming

While NLP primarily focuses on regulating, overseeing, and modifying our cognitive processes to foster constructive mental states that enhance our overall welfare and achievement, it also encompasses distinct disciplines that explore the methods by which we can perceive, influence, and adapt the individuals in our proximity. This bifurcation between scholarly pursuit and practical application frequently leads to the conflation of NLP with manipulative techniques and extrasensory perception. Certainly, it would be implausible to expect that one could simply touch one's finger to another individual's head and instantaneously gain insight into their thoughts and secrets. As of yet, such a portrayal of mind control exists solely within the realm of motion pictures. Nevertheless, NLP affords us with a repertoire of efficacious and validated techniques that enable us to enhance our comprehension and interaction with individuals in our vicinity. When we enhance our capacity to effectively communicate and engage with individuals in a specific manner, we gain the potential to exert the desired influence over these individuals. NLP provides us with the means to exert a particular form of influence over individuals we engage in communication with. Through deliberate gestures, we can effectively establish a sense of ease, prompting them to disclose information that they might otherwise withhold. A judicious application of physical contact can engender feelings of reassurance, fostering a greater receptiveness to our suggestions. Additionally, tailoring our approach to align with an individual's personal preferences can facilitate their openness towards embracing our own viewpoints, beliefs, ideas, and opinions.

Influencing through communication

The capacity to exert influence over others, utilizing Neuro-Linguistic Programming (NLP) techniques, derives from effective communication. And should our intention be to exert an influence on others, be it to alter their perspective, advocate for an alternative stance, or prompt specific behaviors, it is reasonable to assert that we must possess the capacity for exemplary verbal communication, correct? Maturingly, it transpires that the efficacy of our persuasion rests predominantly on the recipients themselves—how we encourage their receptivity, transmit our message with precision, and stimulate their inclination to adopt viewpoints akin to ours. It can be assumed that engaging someone and capturing their interest is contingent upon the subject matter at hand. However, in reality, our ability to effectively communicate and have an impact is predicated on the perceptions and emotions of others during our interaction. As a result, natural language processing (NLP) posits that our capacity to exert influence over others is contingent not upon oral communication, but rather upon:

1. Physical communication
2. Our capacity to attentively listen and exhibit genuine interest
3. How we adapt our communication to align with an individual's preferred modalities.

Environmental

In contrast to biological factors (nature), the impact of environmental factors (nurture) appears to be more nuanced and constitutes a minor, yet still noteworthy, source of variability in individual differences pertaining to the development of triad dark traits. The substantial variance in the three traits of the dark triad (narcissism = 0.41, Machiavellianism = 0.30, psychopathy = 0.32) can be accounted for by the impact of unique or non-shared environmental factors (with definitions and mathematical derivation previously provided in the "Origins" subsection). Only Machiavellianism (r = 0.39) displayed a statistically significant correlation with a shared environmental factor. Although there is a requirement for establishing the foundations, certain researchers have interpreted that the latter discovery (alongside the relatively minor inheritance observed in the previous section) implies that Machiavellianism, as a component of the dark triad, is primarily influenced by experiential factors. This concept of the modifiability of Machiavellianism is logical primarily when a slight variance can be ascribed to genetic factors, while a larger variance should be attributed to factors other than genetics, which have traditionally been defined as environmental in nature.

The theory of evolution can also provide deeper insights into the emergence of the obscure characteristics of the triad. It has been posited that evolutionary conduct encompasses not solely the cultivation of character within the realm of the dark triads, but also the flourishing of such personalities. Indeed, it has been identified that individuals who exhibit traits associated with the dark triad personality are capable of achieving considerable success within society. Nevertheless, this success tends to be transient in nature. The primary evolutionary disagreement among the various schools of thought pertaining to the attributes of the dark triad underscores the strategies of coupling. This topic pertains to the notion of life history strategy. The concept of life history theory posits that individuals exhibit variations in reproductive strategies. The focus on mating is referred to as the "fast life" strategy, whereas the focus on parenting is termed the "slow reproduction" strategy. There is compelling evidence to suggest that the traits associated with the dark triad exhibit a correlation with rapid life history strategies. However, it is worth noting that certain findings have been inconsistent, and not all three characteristics of the dark triad have been found to be associated with this particular strategy. An attempt has been made to provide a more comprehensive analysis by examining features with a higher degree of intricacy in order to elucidate some of these contradictory findings. These scholars have uncovered that while certain elements of the dark triad are associated with an accelerated life strategy, other components exhibit a correlation with less rapid reproductive strategies.

Latent aspects in relation to disturbances.

Typically, medical practitioners regard two of the characteristics (narcissism and psychopathy) as pathological, necessitating intervention and inherently undesirable. These traits are often socially condemned or personally counterproductive. Nevertheless, there are those who contend that maladaptive qualities can be accompanied by adaptive ones. The recent discourse has shed light on the evolutionary viewpoint, which posits that the dark triad embodies distinct approaches to mating. At least one local adaptation is required due to its prevalence in the gene pool.

The inherent characteristics manifested in students and communities also reveal themselves in their day-to-day interactions. In fact, noticeable levels of these traits can even be discerned among individuals who generally exhibit harmonious conduct in their daily routines. Even within these samples, the research demonstrates associations with aggression, racism, and bullying among various forms of social aversion.

Narcissism was discussed in the literary works of Sigmund Freud, while psychopathy was first examined as a clinical diagnosis in Herve Cleckley's initial writings in 1941, notably through the publication of The Mask of Sanity. In light of the conceptual framework incorporating narcissism and psychopathy, along with the inclusion of self-report assessments suitable for the general population, these individuals can now be examined at the subclinical level. The estimated prevalence rates of subclinical and clinical psychopathy in the general population are approximately 1% and 0.2% respectively. Regrettably, it appears that there is a lack of dependable assessments regarding the prevalence of clinical or subclinical narcissism in the general population.

Regarding empirical research, the study of psychopathy did not emerge as a field of inquiry until the 1970s, when Robert Hare began his endeavors by developing the Psychopathy Checklist (PCL) and conducting a comprehensive review known as the PCL-R. Hare highlights in his book, Unconsciously, that requesting psychopaths to introspect on psychologically significant matters may not reliably yield accurate or unbiased data.

However, recent endeavors have been undertaken to validate the psychological condition within the autonomous learning mechanisms of victimization in the dimensional realm, such as through the implementation of Levenson's primary and secondary psychopathic scales and the psychopathic personality inventory.

Moreover, the extent of self-sustaining psychopathy.

In a similar manner, the evaluation of narcissism necessitated clinical interviews until Raskin and Hall developed the widely recognized "Inventory of the narcissistic personality" in 1979.

Multiple additional measures have arisen from the NPI which aim to offer alternative methods for evaluating personality disorder through self-reporting.

Additionally, novel methodologies have been devised to examine the phenomenon of "pathological" narcissism in contrast to the commonly perceived "great" narcissism that the INP metric purportedly assesses.

Machiavellism has not been recorded in any iteration of the Diagnostic and Statistical Manual of Mental Disorders (DSM) in relation to psychological disorders.

It was regarded exclusively as a construct of personality.

The initial disclosed iteration of Mach-IV continues to be the most extensively employed in scholarly investigations.

Chapter 4. Attain Optimum Wellness through Neuro-Linguistic Programming

Utilizing anchors as a means to acquire motivation.

Health programs typically involve a comprehensive approach and require several months to complete. It is not astonishing that numerous individuals discontinue their participation shortly after a few sessions due to a decline in their motivation. Maintaining good health necessitates making lifestyle modifications, which often prove to be challenging endeavors.

Prior to commencing, it is imperative to firmly establish oneself in the appropriate mindset by implementing the methodologies elucidated in the initial chapter. Several states that are often suggested include determination, motivation, and patience. Depending on your personal preference, you have the option to utilize either the basic anchors, collapsing anchors, or chaining anchors.

Additionally, one can employ the technique of anchoring to alleviate sensations such as cravings by merging the state of hunger with the sense of satiety.

Modeling excellence

In every domain, each of us harbors individuals we hold in high regard and strive to emulate. We hold them in high esteem due to their exceptional competence in their field of expertise. Each of them possesses distinct strategic approaches to achieve success.

Modeling is akin to mentorship, where one utilizes another individual as a source of inspiration to emulate. It requires adopting a perspective that allows for a deep understanding of the thoughts and actions of another individual by immersing oneself in their perspective. Once you have obtained consent to emulate the individual you hold in high regard, it is imperative to engage in meaningful dialogue with them to discern their thought processes and actions. In the event that direct access to the person becomes unattainable, alternative means such as online resources can be explored (to be elaborated on shortly).

The process commences by diligently examining the subject, discerning the tactics employed to achieve their success (Druckman, 2004). For the purpose of this exercise, we shall employ the instance of weight reduction. Modeling can also find application in numerous contexts, encompassing the realm of sports training, public speaking preparations, and even in the realm of parenting.

Psychological Influence Through Neuro-Linguistic Programming For Fostering And Enhancing Romantic Partnerships

In order to comprehend the synergy between NLP and mind control, it is imperative to first gain a comprehensive understanding of mind control in isolation.

What is Mind Control?

Mental manipulation refers to the state wherein an individual or external influence exerts control over an individual's cognitive processes and behavioral patterns. This can be accomplished by accessing one's mental faculties through intentional behaviors and verbal expressions in order to mobilize them to accomplish tasks on one's behalf. One might inquire as to the feasibility of exerting control over an individual's thoughts and mental processes. Consequently, the response to this inquiry affirms that it is indeed feasible. One may hold the presumption that accessing the actual brain is the means to achieve this purpose; however, it entails a psychological rather than a physical approach in reality.

An effective approach or illustration can be found in the utilization of hypnosis, a method characterized by one's ability to access the subconscious realm of the mind. The subconscious component of the dominant realm of the psyche. The remaining components encompass the conscious, which constitutes the most diminutive segment of the brain, along with the pre-conscious, situated in the intermediate region of the brain. The subconscious mind accesses the majority of past memories. Upon accessing it, individuals possess the ability to essentially alter someone's present state due to an abundance of unresolved inquiries. Unresolved inquiries are the primary components that shape the historical narrative, exerting an influence on current circumstances once their resolutions are obtained.

Engaging the subconscious mind is a therapeutic strategy commonly applied in the field of psychotherapy, with particular emphasis in the realm of psychoanalysis. Psychoanalysis is a therapeutic modality intended for addressing issues that extend beyond the present moment. Psychoanalysis was initially conceived by Sigmund Freud and subsequently adapted by Erick Erickson. The objective of this therapeutic approach was to shed light on past experiences. This somehow shows mind-controlling. One might inquire regarding the intended meaning or sense behind the statement. The aforementioned concept implies that the previously ambiguous past can now be comprehended, leading to the possibility of awakening and manipulating the brain for various purposes at the discretion of others.

NLP , or Neuro-Linguistic Programming, encompasses a sophisticated system of communication that is primarily mediated by the human mind, specifically discerned through the analysis of brainwave patterns. These intricate processes ultimately culminate in the comprehension and transmission of information via a special code. In the preceding chapter, NLP has been elucidated and proven highly efficacious in addressing cognitive challenges stemming from the intricacies of brain neurology, to put it succinctly. This approach to neurological programming permits the examination and comprehension of the human mind on a broader, more comprehensive level. What are the correlations between NLP and the manipulation of the mind?

The matter concerning mind control and neuro-linguistic programming is straightforward. The modus operandi of their collaboration is not an enigma. The field of NLP communication pertains to the psychological comprehension of the human mind, whereas mind control refers to the means by which the mind or brain is influenced to adhere to specific directives. That fundamentally derives from its nomenclature. In what manner, then, are they interconnected? Mind control can be defined as the process by which the cognitive faculties of an individual are subjected to a certain set of instructions or information which they are compelled to adhere to. NLP facilitates this capability by utilizing encoded messages as a medium of communication, enabling the transmission and reception of information. These encrypted communications are what facilitate the reception of the message by the mind, subsequently leading to the body's adherence and response.

NLP Strategies for Conquering Social Anxiety Disorders

Perspectives on the curability of social phobia through the application of NLP techniques differ among individuals. Nevertheless, it remains an undeniable fact that the treatment of social phobia through a singular technique that guarantees a complete and permanent cure, including the implementation of NLP , is unattainable. The rationale behind this stems from the observation that social phobia is not strictly classified as a phobia. Social phobia can be defined as an anxiety disorder masquerading as an irrational apprehension. This is the exact rationale behind the designation of the term 'phobia' as social anxiety. In order to surmount social phobia, it is imperative to first identify the triggering factor responsible for this condition. For instance, you may feel comfortable socializing with your peers at the nearby pub. Nonetheless, it is possible that you may encounter elevated levels of unease in a different social setting where you lack familiarity with any individuals present. It is imperative to locate the triggering stimulus of the phobia. It would be beneficial to maintain a written record of distinct social circumstances and the corresponding emotional responses they incite.

Furthermore, it is important to highlight that a significant underlying factor contributing to social anxiety/phobia is the level of self-assurance an individual possesses, or the absence thereof. As an illustration, one can experience feelings of anxiety during a social gathering due to being present in an unfamiliar social milieu surrounded by individuals who exude a higher level of education or extensive travel experience than oneself. This implies that the primary source of most problems pertaining to social phobia arises from one's self-perception.

Upon the revelation of your stimulus, proceed to establish an internal mechanism to cope with said stimulus. For instance, a considerable proportion of individuals afflicted with social phobia observe that it arises from an internal dialogue or mental imagery in which Murphy's Law is manifested, leading to a scenario where every possible mishap occurs. Individuals who struggle with social interactions often tend to construct negative self-perceptions in the minds of their counterparts during social gatherings. This ultimately results in heightened discomfort during social occasions and a pervasive aversion towards any social gatherings that demand one's withdrawal from their comfort zone. It is a fact that your behavior is influenced by your level of comfort or discomfort in a social situation. If one experiences unease in the presence of others, it is highly likely that said individuals will also feel discomfort in one's company. Trigger identification is the fundamental component of any NLP methodology. Presented herein is an NLP exercise that has the potential to illuminate your subconscious workings and surmount social phobia.

Exercises in NLP for the Treatment of Social Anxiety Disorder

Once an individual has identified their social trigger, it becomes comparatively simple to discover an NLP technique that proves effective for said trigger. I assert this statement due to the fact that various triggers necessitate diverse NLP methodologies. As a case in point, should your social phobia stem from matters concerning confidence and self-perception, you may consider attempting this exercise geared towards boosting your self-assurance.

Exercise for enhancing confidence in the domain of natural language processing

In order to execute this exercise, assume an upright position and transition into a stabilized physical state. Please gently close your eyes and calmly regulate your breathing. Envision yourself in the presence of your own image. Envision a version of yourself who exudes utmost confidence, just as you desire. You have the ability to imbue within your visualized self the qualities and characteristics exhibited by other individuals who have achieved great success. Please make a note of the alterations seen in your counterpart. The enhancement of confidence leads to an increase in one's stature. Envision a grand and striking image in order to make the alterations in posture and mood evident. Envision the profound self-assurance coursing within this alternate persona, as it animates their veins and imbues them with a heightened sense of well-being. Engage in this exercise until the alternate version of yourself attains a high degree of self-assurance. Once you feel prepared, envision yourself positioned behind your alternate self and smoothly transition into their being, seamlessly adorning them as an additional layer. Experience the influence of their body language, as it aligns with yours, facilitating the transfer of their emotions, enthusiasm, and self-assurance onto you. With such an air of assurance enveloping you, envision yourself standing in front of an audience and receiving a resounding standing ovation. Bask in the acclaim bestowed upon you, observing keenly which area of your physique resonates most powerfully with the newfound self-assurance. Does it originate in your mind or in your abdominal region? What is the subsequent course of action? If it is within your capacity, endeavor to restore the confidence to its original abode, whereupon you shall perceive its augmentation in strength. Please continue to perform this exercise as frequently as necessary or until the sensation becomes unbearable. If the source of your social trigger pertains to an internally generated auditory perception, you may consider engaging in this exercise designed to facilitate the transformation of your emotional response when confronted with a distressing recollection.

As previously mentioned, the issue of social phobia is multifaceted and necessitates a great deal of commitment. Hence, should the aforementioned exercise prove unsuccessful initially, refrain from hastily regarding it as a fraudulent activity. Make another attempt and you may achieve success on the subsequent try.

The Potential Transformation Of Your Life Through NLP

After completing the NLP courses, it became evident that I would never accept anything less than exceptional, particularly when it pertains to pursuing a career that I detested. It was my aspiration and determination that influenced the decision factors for me. I have not, up to this point, reflected upon my decision to resign from my employment, primarily owing to the substantial assistance and encouragement that I received from my spouse. Currently, I am immensely pleased with my current employment situation as it provides me with a significantly higher remuneration compared to my previous occupation, despite the fact that I am now working fewer hours.

An additional advantageous aspect is that it enables me to confidently engage in large gatherings without experiencing shyness or anxiety. Moreover, I have embarked upon confronting my fears while attaining the long-awaited inner and outer tranquility that I have sought for an extended duration. I would like to take this opportunity to inform everyone that miracles have been occurring, and I am deeply grateful for your contributions towards them.

May I inquire about the details of your personal life?

The aforementioned quote serves as but one of numerous testimonials attesting to the profound transformative impact that NLP has had upon individuals' lives. I receive daily correspondence of this nature, eliciting an enlivened response within me. However, simultaneous encounters with information pertaining to the existence of individuals opposed to Natural Language Processing (NLP) also come to my attention.

It is widely acknowledged that NLP or Neuro-linguistic programming has emerged as a highly contested topic. Although it is indisputable that NLP holds value in the realms of business, education, coaching, and personal development, it continues to face criticism from those who perceive it as overrated and devoid of practical utility. These critiques are commonly voiced by individuals with no prior experience or expertise in the field of NLP . The primary cause for the abundant negative feedback is the ongoing research and debate surrounding Neuro-linguistic Programming, as it is a field of study that remains incompletely explored within the scientific community. Therefore, the query at hand is: Does NLP hold intrinsic value and possess the capability to truly facilitate a transformative experience in one's life?

I feel obligated to caution you, before you proceed any further on this subject.

In reality, there exists no absolute truth, but only one's subjective perception of it.

I often utter these words immediately prior to commencing my training sessions. Individuals who endorse the practice of NLP will discover that in addition to the methods employed, NLP also imparts the mindset or disposition required to effect change and observe outcomes.

The concept of curiosity is instructed in the field of NLP .

In Neuro-Linguistic Programming, the concept of maintaining an open mind is emphasized.

The concept of flexibility is imparted in the field of NLP .

Understanding the concept of NLP may appear challenging since its principles are not easily observable. However, one can rely on models to gain insights. It ultimately rests with the individual as to whether or not they choose to embrace these models.

Individuals who possess a sufficient level of maturity and openness to indulge their curiosity are most likely to achieve optimal outcomes by implementing the acquired insights from NLP .

"The intellect, akin to a parachute, operates solely when it is unfurled." - Dr. Kranser

Rather than harboring skepticism towards NLP , the emphasis lies on actualizing NLP and investing diligent effort to ensure its effectiveness.

Students enrolled in the field of Natural Language Processing will acquire the skills necessary to employ a mindset that has proven to be advantageous in their studies. They shall acquire knowledge regarding how their perception of self can lead to transformation. Instruction will also cover the significance of life, spirituality, professional pursuits, interpersonal connections, physical wellness, and holistic health. It revolves around acquiring the knowledge of transforming their automatic thought processes into something more adaptable to their personal habits, thus converting unproductive reactions into productive ones.

Negative thoughts, limitations, and emotions shall be dispelled, alongside obstacles and fear, for which individuals shall be instructed on effective coping strategies. Self-validation and the ability to grant forgiveness to others will also be instructed, along with cultivating a sense of contentment and acceptance of oneself and establishing future objectives and achieving them. Similar to manifesting extraordinary outcomes within their own lives.

Although there remains limited scientific evidence substantiating the efficacy of NLP , there exists a substantial body of testimonials providing compelling evidence of its effectiveness. The arrival of that time shall solely transpire once scientists decipher the means to quantify achievement, contentment, and joy.

Fundamentally, NLP primarily revolves around the fundamental tenets of mind management and cognition enhancement, which, unquestionably, hold considerable significance when it pertains to cultivating personal well-being and achieving success in various aspects of life.

Thus, can NLP truly possess the capacity to transform one's life? It ultimately lies within the discretion of the individual as to whether they choose to do so or not.

Brainwashing Techniques

Delve into methodologies that will aid you in locating the appropriate responses to the inquiries that require your attention. In contemporary times, it has become customary for marketers to employ persuasive techniques and mitigate any potential unease associated with sales transactions to enhance customer satisfaction.

One can consider the concept of psychological manipulation, a phenomenon typically depicted in motion pictures, but rarely encountered in scientific literature. The manner in which the process of brainwashing is carried out involves a strategy of assimilation into one's consciousness. Alternatively, this can be described as a situation where one expresses remorse for a particular action or moment, and gradually weakens a procedure until it eventually fails.

However, in actuality, the phenomenon of brainwashing does not necessarily conform to one's imagination. Given that any action you must take in order for another individual to communicate is incorrect.

Language serves as the foundation of our endeavors, as it is the medium through which we combine and disseminate ideas, expressions, and explanations. It serves as an indication of our individual apprehension of the prevailing reality.

However, it is merely a hint. And subsequently, it diverges from what is observed in our current state of reality. "For instance, numerous aspects of our experiences are omitted when we engage in conversation." Despite our best efforts to be thorough, it may prove challenging to enumerate all of our reasons. Subsequently, we discover an aspect of our existence. Additionally, we have deliberated certain matters that, if feasible, indicate not only our awareness of specific particulars, but also our comprehension of additional specifics. Subsequently, we shall engage in a series of activities, alongside others present, as part of our experiential endeavors.

This entire sequence is impeccable; however, it represents the highest quality content available on our website and remarkably functions exceptionally well despite the various challenges you encounter.

Indeed, this option is highly appropriate for our needs, as it also facilitates the establishment of connections by providing us with an opportunity to engage in meaningful eye contact. Alternatively, we can engage in conversation with other ethereal entities.

Given the phenomena of generations, distortions, and omissions that transpire within language, it is possible that we might clandestinely infiltrate the thoughts of others.

Hence, the influence exerted on minds and issues by language is a potent force.

NLP

A common inquiry often posed by individuals pertains to the nature of NLP : what exactly does it entail? NLP , in essence, refers to Neuro-Linguistic Programming. It embodies a methodology that presents individuals with a wide array of tools and strategies essential for effectively managing the complexities and possibilities of life. It is an applied field of study that aims to translate theoretical knowledge into tangible outcomes.

Essentially, Natural Language Processing (NLP) entails the examination of effective approaches and the specific contexts in which they are effective.

Let us deconstruct the field of NLP by examining its constituent words to enhance our understanding.

Neuro pertains to the physiological network that comprises the body's nervous system. The functioning of our nervous system is subject to the influence of the information we encounter through each of our senses. By acquiring the ability to effectively process information, we will enhance our listening skills and heighten our powers of observation. By cultivating a greater receptiveness towards our own emotions as well as those of others, our cognitive faculties will be endowed with superior data, thereby enabling us to reach optimal decisions for our personal growth. As a consequence, our ability to communicate will be enhanced, both at a subconscious and conscious level.

Linguistic deals with language. As our level of awareness increases, we gain a comprehensive understanding of vocabulary, linguistic structure, as well as the auditory elements of speech including rhythm, vocal intonation, and tempo. The insights derived from this knowledge enhance our decision-making processes and facilitate both unconscious and conscious communication.

Programming pertains to the establishment of regular patterns or routines. All individuals tend to acquire tendencies, wherein certain habits prove beneficial while others may not be as advantageous. NLP will impart knowledge on the cultivation and utilization of beneficial habits while discarding unproductive tendencies.

Creating Reality

A principle upheld by NLP is that each individual bears the responsibility of constructing their own perception of reality.

These maps are selectively processed by our neural network, cognitive frameworks, prior encounters, and sensory apparatus. Primarily, the majority of the challenges we encounter stem from our perception of the world rather than the inherent nature of the world itself. This corresponds to confirmation bias, cognitive dissonance, worldview, and cognitive frameworks.

If we possessed the capacity to enhance our reception and assimilation of sensory input, we would consequently have the capability to enhance our overall level of performance.

Adding Structure

It is imperative that we exhibit mindfulness towards the emotions, auditory perceptions, and visual observations of others. Having the capacity to comprehend our senses and their impact on both ourselves and others will enable us to cultivate tactics that will govern our conduct.

NLP is providing guidance and direction to both others and ourselves. It does not involve coercion, deception or explicit instruction. It pertains to discerning what is advantageous and beneficial for all parties involved.

Taking into consideration all of the aforementioned points, I present my formal definition of NLP as follows: 'NLP investigates the realm of human behavior, communication, and cognition.' This approach facilitates the enhancement of our performance across a diverse range of activities. We subsequently impart the knowledge we have acquired to other individuals.

Benefits of NLP

Assists in forging a connection with your personal motivation, core values, and overarching purpose.

Your life will attain greater fulfillment and success.

Your work performance shall witness enhancement. You could potentially initiate the establishment and operation of your very own enterprise.

You will cultivate improved interpersonal dynamics in both your personal and professional spheres.

You will cultivate improved and wholesome routines.

You will surmount obstacles and continually acquire new proficiencies.

You are poised to find great enjoyment on your personal quest of self-discovery and growth throughout the course of your life.

Needed Attributes

No specific expertise is required to commence the exploration of NLP . Possessing a gentle, intense, lively, and inquisitive demeanor is advantageous, though not obligatory. In order to ascertain desirable outcomes in the pursuit of acquiring knowledge on natural language processing (NLP), it is of great advantage to possess qualities such as sincerity, transparency, audacity, and ambition.

NLP History

NLP , or Neuro-Linguistic Programming, was developed approximately four decades ago by John Grinder and Richard Bandler. They gained valuable experience and acquired knowledge through their collaboration with renowned figures such as Fritz Perls, Virginia Satir, and Milton Erickson. All of these individuals demonstrate exceptional aptitude in the field of therapy and psychiatry during their respective eras. They opted to explore an alternative methodology. Their objective was to effect tangible transformations rather than merely formulating another theoretical construct.

Grinder and Bandler sought to ascertain the methodologies employed by highly skilled individuals, delineate the modus operandi employed during these endeavors, and decipher the actions undertaken in the process. They developed methodologies to emulate these strategies, thereby enabling others to reproduce them. This marked the inception of the initial NLP prototype.

They consistently enhanced it and conducted experiments on their participants. Upon disseminating knowledge of its advantages, NLP commenced proliferating across various domains such as commerce, athletics, creative pursuits, mentorship, and every facet of human undertakings.

Robert Dilts can be regarded as one of the forerunners in the field of NLP . He continues to excel in his efforts to support entrepreneurs in the renowned technological hub of Silicon Valley. His logical frameworks prove to be advantageous for both enterprises and individuals. Each level holds its own significance, as well as the coherence between them. There exists a singular level that can be deemed as the optimal point for the progression of every individual or enterprise. Please examine this breakdown:

Purpose:

What do you want?

What contributions would you like to make to others?

Identity:

Who are you?

Beliefs and values:

What are your perspectives on the nature of the world?

What are your personal convictions regarding your own identity?

What holds significance in your life?

What is the reason for your behavior?

Capabilities:

How do your strategies manifest?

What is your approach to developing a strategic plan?

What are your abilities and proficiencies?

Behavior:

What measures do you undertake?

What do you do?

Environment:

At what time and location do you engage in your activities?

What Factors Contribute To Your Inability To Achieve Weight Loss?

If, despite engaging in the exercise described in the preceding chapter, one finds it challenging to cultivate self-love, it is apparent that there exists a deeply ingrained belief that acts as an impediment. Our perception of the world is shaped by the beliefs we hold. One's beliefs have a profound influence on the accomplishment of their life. The attainment or non-attainment of an individual hinges upon the conviction harbored within their subconscious cognition.

Many individuals lack awareness of the fact that they are functioning within a set of beliefs. Your beliefs have an impact on your cognitive processes, emotional responses, and behavioral patterns. The influence of one's beliefs on their self-perception is of utmost significance. Belief can be defined as an individual's personal conviction in the veracity of a particular notion. Our current state is a direct result of our deeply held convictions. Our actions are influenced by our set of beliefs. One of the factors contributing to individuals' ongoing struggle with maintaining weight loss over the long term is the presence of limiting beliefs. If you maintain the conviction that you are incapable of losing weight, your subconscious will inevitably adopt corresponding behaviors to validate this conviction.

A conviction is established when a profound sentiment is experienced, and the subconscious mind subsequently perceives and comprehends the event or encounter. The majority of beliefs are forged during our childhood years. As previously delineated, the pivotal determinant, commonly referred to as our cognitive sieve, tends to be formed during the period of 6-8 years and attains optimum refinement by approximately 10-12 years of age. Throughout that time period, the subconscious mind autonomously construed occurrences or encounters. Over the course of those years, the subconscious mind arrived at a conclusion regarding the event we had encountered. Please do not have excessively high expectations for this interpretation, as it was generated by the subconscious mind, which was still in a state of youthful innocence and naivety.

As an illustration, it is worth noting that a young male encountered ridicule from his acquaintances subsequent to his vocal performance. The male child's unconscious mental state perceived, "I was subjected to ridicule." My vocal performance is not in harmony. I cannot sing. I have lost interest in participating in singing activities.\\\" The boy experienced feelings of sadness, leading to the eventual establishment of a belief. The young boy ceased his singing activities due to the profound impact of a belief that strongly influenced his behavior. His conviction was centered around the apprehension of experiencing humiliation and ridicule upon performing. Consequently, should he be compelled to do so, his subconscious mind would activate mechanisms to prevent him from singing altogether, potentially manifesting in nervous behavioral patterns.

Convictions exert a pervasive influence on various facets of our lives, encompassing domains like financial matters, health status, interpersonal connections, and more. When we hold a conviction of truth, our emotions and actions align with this conviction. Regardless of an individual's diligent efforts, if they hold the belief that "I am poor," attaining wealth will remain an unachievable feat. If one holds the belief that life represents a constant strife, it will indeed manifest as such. If one maintains the belief that acquiring money is a challenging endeavor, then indeed money will prove to be elusive. Should you hold the conviction that attaining a slender physique is an insurmountable feat, then indeed, the achievement of a slim body would remain unattainable. Your belief system determines the essence and trajectory of your life.

The process of weight loss encompasses more than just the attributes of discipline and willpower. The primary challenge encountered while attempting to achieve weight loss does not typically arise from the presence of enticing foods or strenuous exercises, but rather from the emergence of limiting beliefs that hinder progress. Recognizing the possibility of achieving weight loss is a significant stride. One must alter their belief before altering their outcome. The power of conviction lies in its ability to manifest reality. I am confident that you are familiar with the expression, "One's belief in their ability to achieve or not achieve something profoundly influences the outcome." Your conviction shall exert an influence over your demeanor, conduct, emotional well-being, and physiological condition, thereby dictating the outcomes you achieve. Constraining beliefs restrict our range of options or capacities to a certain extent.

There was an instance involving a young girl who developed obesity due to the repeated remarks made by her parents and relatives during her childhood, such as "You're so fat, yet so adorable!" Her subconscious mind internalized these messages, forming the belief that being overweight equated to cuteness. Her desire to appear endearing ultimately resulted in her becoming overweight.

Additionally, there was an instance wherein a woman experienced weight gain as a result of a traumatic incident during her youth, involving a violation committed by an individual she had placed her trust in. The incident invoked an interpretation within her subconscious that posited her beauty as the reason for the attack. Her subconscious mind has inherently predisposed her to possess a larger physique, resulting in a less aesthetically pleasing appearance, a manifestation that serves as a means of self-preservation. If she possesses a larger body size, there would likely be a diminished level of interest from potential suitors.

Do those instances exhibit logical coherence? It is illogical, at least based on conscious reasoning. Beliefs do not stem from a rational framework of concepts. The subconscious mind is unaware of principles of logic, rationality, and even basic common sense. For example, phobia. For phobias such as acrophobia, ophidiophobia, and crocodilophobia, the fear is understandable, as these stimuli possess inherent levels of danger. However, one must also consider phobias of seemingly harmless objects such as feathers, plaster, balloons, and perfumes, as they appear to lack logical explanation.

The subconscious mind is unaware of whether it is logical or not. The contents with which we imbue our subconscious mind have the potential to exert considerable influence over the patterns of our cognition and behavior, irrespective of their logical coherence. This is the manner in which the subconscious mind operates. That exemplifies the functioning of the belief. For a deeper understanding of the relationship between belief and its impact on personal accomplishments, I would recommend perusing my earlier literary work titled "Change Your Belief Change Your Life: A Practical Guide on Altering Your Restrictive Beliefs, Realizing Your Objectives, and Cultivating the Life of Your Desire."

Understanding the underlying factors contributing to your weight gain will facilitate your attainment of a healthier body mass. Both aforementioned cases are factual instances. After identifying the root cause of their weight gain, they commenced a process of weight loss. Undoubtedly, not all instances exhibit the same degree of extremity.

Subconscious mind is very powerful. Any notions that are deposited within the depths of your subconscious mind will inevitably manifest into actuality. The extent to which your weight loss endeavor proves successful is contingent upon your thoughts and beliefs. "If you are of the mindset that: By any chance, if you happen to harbour any thoughts such as: In the event that you possess any notions along the lines of: In case you are inclined to think along the lines of:

I find that whenever I successfully shed pounds, I inevitably regain them.

I consume very little, yet my body weight remains consistent.

I am unable to achieve weight loss due to a lack of available time for physical exercise.

The process of weight loss is predominantly determined by my genetic makeup, leaving me with limited control over it.

Weight loss is a challenging endeavor to achieve. Attempting to avoid it is even more difficult."

If such is your perception, that shall be your reality. Should you hold the belief that you possess excess weight, it is likely that you will indeed possess excess weight. If you maintain the conviction that you are incapable of achieving weight loss, you will indeed be unable to achieve weight loss. Should you hold the belief that the task of maintaining your ideal weight is arduous, you will indeed find it challenging to achieve and sustain said weight. If you hold the belief that your excess weight is primarily attributed to genetic factors and thus it is unlikely for you to achieve weight loss, then it is an outcome of your conviction.

Certain beliefs have the capacity to empower individuals, while others have the tendency to place limitations on their potential. Empowering beliefs are instrumental in enabling us to effectively pursue our desired objectives. Though the prevalence of limiting beliefs poses significant challenges, they impede our progress and exacerbate the complexities of life.

Constraining beliefs precipitate self-defeating conduct. Eliminating restrictive beliefs is imperative in attaining any desired outcome, including the attainment of weight loss. In order to ascertain whether you hold empowering or limiting beliefs regarding weight loss, there is a singular method that can be employed. Consider the scenario wherein you have successfully shed excess weight and attained a trim and desirable physique. Take a moment to envisage this outcome and subsequently, observe the emotional response that arises within you. If you encounter difficulties in envisioning this concept, it may be beneficial to seek visual references by conducting a search for images depicting slender physiques. Subsequently, attempt to mentally project yourself possessing a physique akin to those images. Take notice of the emotional response you experience.

Why emotion? A common fallacy pertaining to beliefs lies in the notion that a belief is merely a cognitive process. Belief transcends mere cognition. Faith is united with an emotional response. Emotion is pure. The sentiment experienced can serve as an indicator of the underlying workings of the subconscious program. Internal cognition or introspection is frequently an inadequate indicator since it can be influenced by the individual's conscious mental processes. Our emotions can provide insights into our thoughts. One can deceive their conscious mind, yet one would be unsuccessful in deceiving the subconscious mind.

If one experiences favorable emotions, such as being motivated, enthused, content, or displaying an immediate desire to achieve the desired physique, then rest assured! There are no hindering beliefs concerning weight loss.

However, if one experiences adverse sentiments such as fear, unwarranted animosity, or a sense of disappointment, it can be indicative of a restrictive belief system. It is imperative that you address this matter, otherwise your endeavors towards weight loss will prove futile. Please refrain from attempting to evade or circumvent these unfavorable emotions. On the contrary, you must deliver them. If one actively refrains from interacting with it, they shall cease to exist momentarily; however, it shall inevitably resurface.

The human intellect bears resemblance to that of a computing device. Once a program has been installed on our computer, it can be uninstalled if it is no longer required. We acquired knowledge of belief in the past due to its practical utility for us. However, should the information or skills prove to be of no utility to us, they can be unacquired. The majority of individuals lack the knowledge of how to effectively relinquish this ingrainment, thereby persisting in its effects and exacerbating the difficulty of their lives. There exists a solitary method that can be utilized to alleviate the negative emotions that manifest due to the presence of a constraining belief. Upon the successful release of negative emotion, the associated limiting belief will naturally dissipate. The technique is EFT.

AN AWFUL LOT

The misuse of funds in a self-centered manner can result in dire consequences. If the universe bestows its wealth upon an individual, that individual should demonstrate the kindness to utilize their good fortune for the betterment of the world and its inhabitants. Financial resources are seldom available without any cost.

Gordon led a life of moderate ordinariness. He was married, possessed a modest vehicle, resided in an ordinary dwelling, and harbored conventional aspirations for his life's purpose.

His aspiration encompassed achieving victory in the lottery. When inquired about the magnitude of his desired winnings, he would simply respond, "A significant sum of money."

Each week, he would purchase his tickets with his regular numbers. However, on one occasion, enticed by the prospect of a significant rollover jackpot, he decided to indulge in a randomly selected ticket.

In short, he emerged triumphant and received a substantial sum of money.

He hastily departed and purchased an expansive residence that included a fully equipped swimming pool. He purchased a high-performance automobile with the intention of impressing everyone. Due to the magnitude of his victory, he elected to retain the funds exclusively for his own benefit. He discerned that his spouse, despite being five years younger than him, exhibited signs of aging. Therefore, he pursued social venues such as bars and clubs where he encountered a romantic partner who was half his age. She possessed exceptional expertise in monetary expenditures and exhibited a high degree of assertiveness. She desired diamonds and gold. She required the most exquisite cuisine from the most esteemed dining establishments, and she expected a compensation every time they engaged in intimate relations.

He possessed a considerable sum of money, and in his perspective, it was entirely justified. He possessed the financial means to engage highly skilled legal professionals, thereby successfully extricating his spouse from his personal affairs at a justifiable expense.

He conjectured that his friends from previous times were exhibiting a sense of detachment towards him, potentially due to harboring feelings of envy towards his affluence. He possessed sufficient financial means to acquire replacement items, regardless.

He grew disinterested in his girlfriend and pursued new companions, who were notably younger and more attractive.

Mona, who served as an investment analyst, provided him with advice on optimizing his expenditure for optimal returns.

After being informed of several successful transactions, he was extremely pleased to allocate all of his savings, assets, and trust into the most exceptional investment opportunity.

Mona informed him that she must embark on a journey to South America in order to guarantee the complete finalization of the agreement. He bid her farewell at the airport, then proceeded to retreat to his spacious residence, indulging in a leisurely swim in his inviting swimming pool before luxuriating in the company of a substantial cigar.

There was a complete absence of communication from Mona; there were no phone calls, no text messages, and no correspondence received. He harbored concerns regarding her well-being.

The sounding of the security gates signaled the arrival of an individual.

He directed his gaze towards the closed-circuit television monitor, where he observed the presence of two individuals dressed in formal attire. He was concerned that an unfortunate event had occurred to the girl who he held in high regard. He let them in.

The bailiffs swiftly removed the man from his residence, confiscated the keys to his vehicle, and left him locked out. He lacked financial stability, a place of residence, and companionship.

He made a phone call to his former spouse and requested assistance. She expressed deep satisfaction upon receiving communication from her former spouse and expressed a willingness to financially support his absence, using the phrase "go to Hell" to articulate her sentiment.

"I earnestly require your presence, as I am deeply devoted to you." He implored. She laughed. I am willing to undertake a task on your behalf. I will provide you with sufficient funds to acquire an additional lottery ticket. You always had a strong desire for a substantial amount of wealth. That is precisely what you have acquired. The monetary prize you obtained has bestowed upon you a wretched existence. I am affording you the opportunity to potentially obtain a greater sum of money, which may prove to be significantly adverse for your circumstances."

She terminated the call and proceeded with her life that fell below the norm.

She had taken the small sum of money provided by her husband's legal representatives and had been generously compensated. She possessed a significant amount of wealth at present.

She greeted her new associate with a warm smile and emitted hearty laughter for a considerable duration before resuming her duties within the animal sanctuary she had acquired.

Metaphors In ZeNLP !

ZeNLP is often referred to as the "Compendium of cognitive processes for the human mind." It comprises a pragmatic and extensive array of instruments that can aid you in understanding and attaining exceptional performance in your respective domain.
• The term Zen originated from the Sanskrit word dhyan, denoting the practice of meditation.
• Neuro is a term that pertains to our neurological system. The neural pathways of our brain can be likened to thoroughfares, while ingrained habits represent well-worn grooves in the mind. Our cognitive processes traverse these neural pathways, typically in an automatic manner. Broadening the range of potential paths to explore can be effortlessly achieved by fostering a heightened consciousness of one's thoughts. (Zen Meditation)

- The term "linguistic" pertains to the language that an individual possesses. Language serves as a vehicle for shaping our internal and external experiences. When employed with mindfulness, language has the potential to broaden one's perspective and enhance one's lived encounters. (Auto-suggestion)
- Programming pertains to our ingrained cognitive patterns or systems. Ideologies or convictions are perpetually embraced, oftentimes without conscious acknowledgment and effortlessly operate on autopilot. The profound fundamental convictions you hold are consistently manifested in the external realm. Gaining consciousness of the underlying programs that influence you can alone be sufficient to instigate transformation, as well as bestow liberation and the ability to exercise choice. (Creative Visualisation)

There exists a notable correlation between the practice of meditation, the recitation of potent mantras, and the use of creative visualization in ancient Indian civilizations from the Vedic era onward, such as amongst the esteemed rishis. Significantly, narratives have significantly contributed to the development of neural connections in our cerebral cortex and shaping the psychological development of Indian children across multiple generations. India possesses a vibrant heritage of narrative transmission, evident through the abundance of teaching stories such as the Jataka tales, Panchatantra, and various other mythological narratives that have been visually depicted in Amar Chitra Katha. A significant number of our renowned narratives have been disseminated to other nations in the Far East and are presently thriving in countries such as Indonesia and Malaysia. As Buddhism gained wider recognition, our collection of moral tales known as the 'Jataka tales' underwent an adaptation that incorporated Japanese influences, ultimately manifesting as Zen stories in the Japanese tradition.

In contemporary times, large-scale multinational corporations of esteemed stature have commonly restated Zen narratives as part of their organizational practices known as Corporate Myth Training (CMT). Through this deliberate approach, these corporations have successfully cultivated renowned anecdotes that serve as the foundation for the development and proliferation of corporate myths. These mythical encounters are intricately integrated into ZeNLP training programs and constitute an essential element in the formation of neural connections within the brain. ZeNLP categorizes this methodology as 'metaphor'. Metaphors enhance the efficacy and proficiency of any training program by simplifying concepts, facilitating easy recollection, and eliciting an emotional response. ZeNLP comprises a method of instruction where Zen narratives are artfully interwoven within corporate training initiatives, heightening efficacy through their resonance with participants and facilitating lasting assimilation within the subconscious cognition of trainees. The stories that our grandmother shares have become a highly sought-after tool among the training strategies employed by prestigious multinational corporations listed on the Fortune 500. One notable aspect of ZeNLP is its ability to induce profound shifts in attitudes by utilizing the narrative form of language. In addition, these modifications are of a lasting nature, a desire cherished by every professional in the field of corporate training.

A senior lady enters a retail establishment and informs the attendant standing at the counter that the tires fail to meet her expectations. She expresses dissatisfaction with their performance and asserts her urgent need for a refund. "May I inquire whether you have indeed procured these items from our establishment?" the employee inquires. "I am absolutely certain," responds the woman. I am well aware that I made the purchase of these tires from this very location. However, the establishment does not offer tires for sale. After conducting a brief inquiry, the employee is informed by his manager that the establishment, which, despite being relatively new, was actually constructed on the premises of a former fuel station. It is highly probable that this is where the woman purchased her tires. Therefore, the employee proceeds to withdraw Rs 500 from the cash drawer, transfers it to the woman, and expresses remorse for the tires not meeting her expectations. He inquires whether there are any additional tasks he can assist her with, and upon her refusal, he bids her farewell with a gracious expression.

We innovatively conceptualized this compelling narrative and leveraged its impact to the fullest in conducting training for a cohort of recent management graduates who had recently joined the customer service department of a retail chain. Narratives possess the ability to intricately manifest their essence through compelling visualization, exerting a profound influence on the audience, irrespective of factual veracity. The manifestation of creativity arises when one spontaneously fabricates a fictional narrative. Nevertheless, the crucial aspect in ZeNLP lies in the ramifications the story possesses. Dr. Milton H. Erickson, a prominent figure in the field of hypnotherapy at a global level, had the ability to induce deep trances in patients simply through narrative storytelling.

Disney employees undergo extensive training to cultivate the ability to craft what they describe as 'magical experiences' for the guests they serve. Presented herein is an anecdote detailing the actions of a Disney employee who successfully achieved said outcome.

An employee working at a Disney theme park observed two women, one engaged in a pose for a photograph while the other made preparations to capture the moment. The Disney cast member approached the duo and kindly volunteered to capture a photograph of them together. The women happily agreed. Several months later, the employee was presented with a letter via his superior. The source of the image can be traced back to one of the women portrayed. Surprisingly, it transpired that the women were siblings who had ceased all communication with one another for several years. Recognizing that the sisters were fatigued by their ongoing conflict, their family collectively contributed to arranging a trip that would facilitate their reconnection and facilitate the resolution of their disputes at 'the happiest place on earth'. The women had an exceptional experience at Disney, which served as a catalyst for the commencement of a new chapter in their relationship. Subsequently, soon after the visit, one of the sisters fell ill and subsequently passed away. The photograph captured by the Disney staff member stood as the sole depiction of the two sisters during their significant excursion of reconciliation. It held profound significance for the surviving sibling, who subsequently composed a letter addressed to Disney, conveying her heartfelt gratitude. Not all narratives originating from Disney exhibit such profound emotional impact.

A Caveman Mind set

Are you acquainted with the term "caveman"?
The ancient forebears of Honolulu are commonly denoted as the Caveman. What activities were undertaken by the prehistoric humans? The cavemen are commonly acknowledged for their adeptness in hunting; indeed, they displayed remarkable prowess as hunters. A primitive human exhibits exceptional acumen, vigilance, and accuracy while engaging in the act of hunting. He possesses a clear understanding of his desired objectives, demonstrating both astuteness in identifying his targets and competence in devising effective strategies to attain his desired outcomes. It is evident that he is devoid of any sense of compassion during the act of hunting. While the male individual engages in the pursuit of sustenance through hunting, the female counterpart remains at the cave premises, diligently attending to the

childcare responsibilities. In her youth, she resided within the confines of the cave. Furthermore, she would attend to the responsibilities of tending to the goats, as well as providing diligent care for the cattle and other domestic animals. She will ensure the proper care and safety of the children, ensuring their well-being. Subsequently, it is her responsibility to make arrangements for nourishment for her spouse. Examine the psychological attributes of the prehistoric woman, as she possesses various cognitive faculties at her disposal. In ancient times, the primary task of the cave dweller was to eliminate the animal, while their female counterparts were engaged in various domestic duties such as maintaining cleanliness, preparing meals, providing care, and offering assistance. As a consequence, the emotional aspect of the male was diminished, whereas that of the female was heightened throughout the entirety of their communal existence. Hence, this is the explanation for her heightened sensitivity.

Furthermore, an additional factor contributing to women's sensitivity lies in their role as mothers. As they carry the baby within their womb, they must consequently prioritize both their own well-being and that of the developing child. Consequently, women often experience an increase in sensitivity. Hence, this constitutes a key rationale why women consistently prioritize the well-being of others. In her capacity as a mother, she possesses the unique ability to discern whether the child's cries stem from physical distress, a desire for attention, discomfort resulting from an insect bite, or any other cause.

It is difficult for individuals of the male gender to grasp the intricacies of such delicate matters, as their emotional reservoirs are often lacking in depth. This served as the fundamental principle upon which the psychological research was conducted. Now let us revisit the present state of our society.

Contemporary society has undergone significant transformations. I would assert that it is the era commonly referred to as the "digital age," wherein the internet exerts considerable influence over various facets of society. In contemporary times, the pace of life has accelerated significantly, rendering money as no longer a predominant obstacle. On the contrary, time has emerged as a paramount challenge for the majority of households. The demands of the past and the requirements of traditional practices are no longer applicable in the present context. Presently, the circumstances have undergone a complete transformation. For modern parents, the difficulty lies in establishing a harmonious equality-based partnership, necessitating a delicate equilibrium between professional commitments and domestic responsibilities for both spouses. In addition, they must attend to the requirements of the children. Everything is fast. The syllabus for children has witnessed a significant augmentation, education is being strongly emphasized, and in contemporary times, parents have had to acquire additional knowledge in order to instruct their children effectively. Additionally, in the event that formal education is lacking, the internet and negative peer influences may serve as conduits to detrimental lifestyles. This poses a grave threat to society, necessitating the provision of appropriate and informed assistance to the internet generation in order to mitigate the proliferation of this social ailment within every household.

Planning outcomes
If your objective in delivering a presentation does not encompass any desired action from your audience, it can be considered a fruitless endeavor that squanders both your time and theirs. If your objective solely involves information transmission, an email has the potential to substitute your presentation. A presentation is an instrument of specialized communication, thus employ it to attain the desired outcome for your purposes. Thoroughly contemplate the additional

value that the presentation brings, beyond any alternative mode of communication.

Even the act of making a decision or forming an opinion can be considered an action, as it necessitates the audience to analyze information and subsequently engage in some form of response. Developing an opinion involves an engaged procedure, much like the act of purchasing an item.

What do I want?

How will the individuals present in this chamber assist me in attaining it?

What tasks or functions do I require them to perform on my behalf?

In what state must they find themselves in order to accomplish that?

When formulating a Well Formed Outcome for your presentation, it is essential to ensure that it remains within your sphere of influence. In the event that you seek comprehension or consensus from the audience, it is important to acknowledge that such outcomes are beyond your direct influence. Consequently, it is imperative to ascertain your own objectives prior to taking action.

A significant number of individuals within organizations engage in delivering presentations aimed at providing information or imparting knowledge to customers. That is beyond your jurisdiction.

When proceeding through successive levels of authority, the initial element within your jurisdiction is your personal state of being. When a harmonious connection is established with the audience, your demeanor will impact their disposition, leading them towards the desirable outcome you intend for them.

In addition to familiarizing yourself with various persuasive techniques, the most straightforward approach to obtain compliance from individuals is by clearly communicating your desires to them. It is crucial to develop the practice of effectively communicating your desires and requirements to others. The last inquiry, commonly known as a "tag question," serves to reinforce the conclusion by typically prompting a favorable response from the majority of obliging and rational individuals. The crucial aspect lies in its ability to induce a reaction, as cultivating an engaged audience is undoubtedly a desired outcome, correct?

If an individual requests something beyond the capabilities of others, they will respond by either clearly stating "no" or responding hesitantly with an ambiguous "erm...OK" that ultimately conveys their negative intent.

Numerous individuals possess apprehensions when it comes to expressing their desires. That is acceptable, as an excessive amount of commotion would ensue if everyone were to express their desires. It is commendable that a significant number of individuals are raised by their parents to embrace the notion that settling for mediocrity, acquiescing to their circumstances, is perceived as positive. This indicates that acquiring desired outcomes can be effortlessly accomplished through direct requests. It is due to the apprehension of others that this approach functions exceptionally well.

And you possess the audacity to pursue your desires without apprehension, do you not?

Certainly, an alternative explanation exists. Envision a scenario wherein the world is replete with individuals who are content, virtuous, benevolent, and altruistic. They are willing to provide assistance, as long as your request does not directly put them at a disadvantage. They possess the desire to offer assistance to you, yet they lack the knowledge or means to do so. By effectively communicating your desires to them, you are facilitating their assistance, thereby leading to their contentment.

In light of everything, one experiences a sense of fulfillment when lending assistance to others, do they not?

Additionally, I strongly recommend commencing each presentation in this manner.

What I am seeking is your contemplation on the significance of this matter to your business. Thus, I kindly request your undivided attention and urge you to pose any inquiries that may aid your comprehension of our potential collaboration. I am eager to know your perspective on this.

In prior years, I collaborated with a client who encountered challenges with internal communication. They convened a bi-monthly board meeting during which they would address all project updates and finalize all critical decisions. The meeting primarily consisted of a two-day series of presentations.

The unfolding scenario can be described as follows: following a project update, a group of individuals would engage in a series of uncomfortable inquiries. These individuals would bring up forgotten aspects, scrutinize the presenter's approach, suggest alternative courses of action, and generally deconstruct the project, leading the presenter to feel besieged by their comments. The speaker would express, "However, all of the aforementioned information was clearly stated in the agenda. Did any of you take the time to peruse it?" Regrettably, it seems that none of the individuals actually acquainted themselves with the contents of the agenda. They were too busy.

A different individual would provide pertinent details for consideration, such as the straightforward matter of purchasing cellular devices. They would thoroughly evaluate tariffs, statistical data, suppliers, and other relevant factors, and subsequently request the board's judicious decision at the conclusion of the presentation. More questions. Have you had a discussion with the supplier in question?" "May I inquire as to the rationale behind your current approach?" "Have you considered engaging in communication with this particular supplier?" "What is the reasoning behind your focus on those specific phones?" "Could you please provide me with the price associated with making a call to another mobile device on that network? The speaker would express, with emphasis, "However, it was clearly stated in the agenda. Did anyone take the time to peruse its contents?" Regrettably, it appears that no one had ever taken the initiative to review the agenda. They were too busy.

With each subsequent meeting, a lack of decision-making, stagnant project progression, and an oppressive anticipation became ingrained among the participants.

The solution was straightforward and easily discernible, and I am confident that you can surmise its nature. The presenters refrained from instructing the audience on listening techniques, nor did they provide directives on the action required from the audience. So every individual in the audience assumed their respective pre-established roles, whether it be succumbing to slumber, engaging in contentious dialogue, highlighting the presenter's lack of preparation, or any other manifestation.

Furthermore, the lack of organization in the presentations resulted in a lack of clarity for the audience regarding the purpose of each subsequent presentation. It is not surprising that they experienced confusion and opted to withdraw to their familiar surroundings.

Instead of their original approach, I instructed them to initiate each presentation with a framing statement, such as:

I hereby provide an update regarding the progress made on my project. I kindly request that no advice or feedback be given at this juncture, as the purpose of this communication is to merely keep you informed.

I shall be delivering a comprehensive presentation on the mobile phone procurement initiative, and subsequently, I kindly request your input on the preferred supplier for our organization.

Informing individuals that "I am providing an update on my project solely for your information at this stage, and no advice or feedback is required" clearly communicates their expected role. On the contrary, the act of presenting an extensive quantity of factual information and subsequently soliciting individuals to make a decision is inherently prone to complications. By clearly articulating your expectations beforehand, individuals will prioritize their focus appropriately and be equipped to render decisions promptly. Consequently, they will abstain from seeking additional time for contemplation or posing complex questions solely to divert attention away from their lack of attentiveness.

Indeed, you have the potential to exceed these expectations. You should ensure that your presentation is additionally concentrated and influential. Using the examples above:

I have come to deliver an update regarding the progress of my project. What information would you require to ensure confident communication regarding the progress of your own teams?

I kindly request that you reach a decision regarding the selection of our mobile phone supplier. What specific information is required from me in order to facilitate the decision-making process?

www.ingramcontent.com/pod-product-compliance
Lightning Source LLC
Chambersburg PA
CBHW050233120526
44590CB00016B/2067